Native
American
Peoples

# CHEYENNE

D. L. Birchfield

Gareth Stevens Publishing
A WORLD ALMANAC EDUCATION GROUP COMPANY

**Please visit our web site at: www.garethstevens.com**
**For a free color catalog describing Gareth Stevens Publishing's list of high-quality books**
**and multimedia programs, call 1-800-542-2595 (USA) or 1-800-387-3178 (Canada).**
**Gareth Stevens Publishing's fax: (414) 332-3567.**

**Library of Congress Cataloging-in-Publication Data**

Birchfield, D. L., 1948-
    Cheyenne / by D. L. Birchfield.
      p. cm. — (Native American peoples)
    Summary: A discussion of the history, culture, and contemporary life of the
Cheyenne Indians.
    Includes bibliographical references and index.
    ISBN 0-8368-3701-0 (lib. bdg.)
    1. Cheyenne Indians—Juvenile literature. [1. Cheyenne Indians. 2. Indians
of North America—Great Plains.] I. Title. II. Series.
E99.C53B57   2003
978.004'973—dc21                        2003045589

First published in 2004 by
**Gareth Stevens Publishing**
A World Almanac Education Group Company
330 West Olive Street, Suite 100
Milwaukee, WI 53212 USA

Produced by Discovery Books
Project editor: Valerie J. Weber
Designer and page production: Sabine Beaupré
Photo researcher: Rachel Tisdale
Native American consultant: Robert J. Conley, M.A., Former Director of Native American
  Studies at Morningside College and Montana State University
Maps and diagrams: Stefan Chabluk
Gareth Stevens editorial direction: Mark Sachner
Gareth Stevens art direction: Tammy Gruenewald
Gareth Stevens production: Beth Meinholz and Jessica L. Yanke

Photo credits: Native Stock: cover, pp. 9 (bottom), 12 (both), 13, 15 (bottom), 16 (both), 17
(top), 18, 19 (both), 20, 22, 23, 24, 26, 27; Corbis: pp. 5, 14, 17 (bottom), 21 (top), 25; North
Wind Picture Archives: p. 6; Peter Newark's American Pictures: pp. 7, 8, 9 (top), 10, 11 (both),
15 (top and middle), 21 (bottom).

Printed in the United States of America

1 2 3 4 5 6 7 8 9 07 06 05 04 03

Cover caption: Four Cheyenne friends gather in Oklahoma. Today's Cheyenne children reflect
both their Native heritage and the American culture.

# Contents

Words that appear in the glossary are printed in
**boldface** type the first time they appear in the text.

# Chapter 1

# Origins

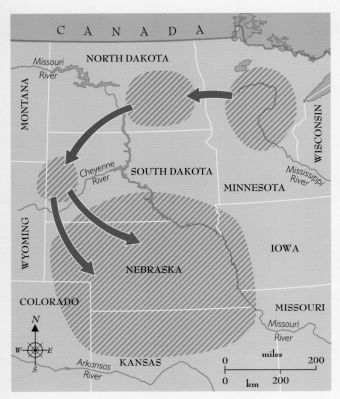

As the red areas on the map show, the Cheyennes first lived in what is now Minnesota, migrating to North Dakota in the 1600s. Pushed southwest to the Black Hills of South Dakota, they became buffalo hunters on the northern Great Plains after 1760.

## Land of the Cheyennes

The Cheyennes are a North American Native people who became one of the most famous tribes of the Great Plains during the nineteenth century. Today, about eight thousand Northern Cheyennes live on the Northern Cheyenne Reservation in Montana. About five thousand Southern Cheyennes live in Oklahoma, mostly on or near the Concho Reservation, which they share with the Southern Arapaho tribe.

The Cheyennes' name for themselves is *Tsetschestahase*, meaning "people who are alike" or "our people." The name *Cheyenne* derives from a Sioux word, *Shai-ena*, meaning "people of an **alien** speech."

## The Cheyenne Origin Story

No one knows exactly how the Cheyennes and other Native American peoples came to North America, but like many cultures, traditional Cheyennes explain their arrival in an origin story. According to this story, all things were formed by a Creator, who made three kinds of people in the far north — hairy people, white people, and red people. The red people followed the hairy people to the south, but the hairy people eventually disappeared. When the red people returned to the north, they found that the white people were gone. The Creator then gave the red people corn to grow and buffalo to hunt.

Some scientists think that Indians may have originally come to North America from Asia, perhaps a long time ago during the Ice Age, if there had been a landmass across the Bering Strait between Alaska and Asia at that time. Others think that Native Americans might have come by boat from Asia.

A Cheyenne in powwow dress at the Red Earth Festival. This large competitive powwow is held each June in downtown Oklahoma City.

## ～ⵡⵡ The Language of the Cheyennes ⵡⵡ～

One of the great language families of North America, the Algonquian language family includes Cheyenne, Ojibwe, Blackfoot, and Shawnee, among many others. The tribes that speak an Algonquian language are widely scattered across North America. They have been separated from each other for a long time since the days in the distant past when they all spoke the same language.

| Cheyenne | Pronunciation | English |
|----------|---------------|---------|
| hetane | hey-than-eh | man |
| mahtse | maht-she | mouth |
| maahe | mah-hey | arrow |
| vaotseva | vah-oht-she-vah | deer |
| netse | neht-she | eagle |
| mahpe | mah-peh | water |
| nahkohe | nah-ko-hey | bear |
| mahtame | mah-tah-meh | food |

# History

French explorer René-Robert Cavelier, Sieur de La Salle. The Cheyennes' first contact with a European was with La Salle in 1680.

## A Woodland People

For hundreds of years, the Cheyennes were a woodland people living in the Great Lakes region in permanent villages. Their lifestyle, based on hunting, fishing, and farming, was similar to that of other woodland peoples.

## Life in the New Land

During the early 1700s, however, the Cheyennes were driven west to the northern Great Plains south of today's Canada by their enemies, the Assiniboins and Ojibwes, and became **nomadic** buffalo hunters. There they met the Sutaio tribe, a people so closely related to them they could understand each others' language. By about 1800, the Sutaios had joined the Cheyenne tribe.

The Cheyennes acquired horses from other Native American groups about 1760, becoming much more mobile, able to follow the buffalo herds and move camp more easily. They soon became a mighty Great Plains tribe.

During the early 1800s, however, American traders brought whiskey to exchange with the Cheyennes for their buffalo robes. **Alcoholism** became a big problem for the tribe.

Hunting buffaloes on horseback was dangerous work requiring great skill. Horses, however, allowed hunters to cover more ground and kill more buffaloes.

## The Cheyenne Bands Separate

The various bands of the Cheyennes became accustomed to living and hunting in different river valleys on the Great Plains. By 1832, the tribe had separated into Northern Cheyennes, who lived mainly in northern Wyoming and southeastern Montana, and Southern Cheyennes, who stayed mainly in the Arkansas and North Canadian River valleys in eastern Colorado, southwestern Kansas, and northwestern Oklahoma.

## War on the Southern Plains

During the first half of the nineteenth century, relations between the Cheyennes and the United States were mostly peaceful.

We kill buffalo by the thousand; our women's hands are sore with dressing the robes; and what do we part with them to the white trader for? We pay them for the white man's fire-water [whiskey], which turns our brains upside down, which makes our hearts black, and renders our arms weak. It takes away our warriors' skill, and makes them shoot wrong in battle. Our enemies, who drink no whiskey, when they shoot, they always kill their foe.

*Porcupine Bear,*
*Cheyenne chief, 1831*

A second Treaty of Fort Laramie was signed in 1868. Here, U.S treaty commissioners are shown with chiefs of the Cheyenne and Arapaho tribes.

In 1849, the U.S. Army established Fort Laramie in eastern Wyoming to protect American settlers traveling across the Great Plains on the Oregon Trail. Cheyennes joined many other Plains tribes in signing the Fort Laramie **Treaty** of 1851, allowing safe passage of the **immigrants** on the trail.

Everything changed, however, when, in 1856, peaceful Cheyennes approaching a wagon on the Oregon Trail in Nebraska were fired on. The Cheyennes fired back, wounding the wagon driver with an arrow. In revenge, soldiers from Fort Kearney, Nebraska, attacked and destroyed a Cheyenne camp, killing eight people. The incident ignited a war with the Southern Cheyennes that would last until the 1880s.

## European Diseases

In 1849, a devastating **epidemic** of **cholera** killed as many as one-half of the Cheyenne people, greatly reducing their power. Throughout Native American history, European diseases killed far more Indians than all other causes combined, including war. European diseases were new to Indians, and it has taken a long time for their bodies to build up a natural resistance to them.

## U.S. Attacks on Peaceful Villages

Some prominent Southern Cheyenne leaders, such as chief Black Kettle, tried to pursue peace with the Americans. However, Colorado Volunteers, under the command of Colonel John Chivington, attacked Black Kettle's peaceful village in eastern Colorado in 1864, killing many women and children in an event called the Sand Creek **Massacre**.

The 1867 Treaty of Medicine Lodge, signed by the Southern Cheyennes, the Kiowas, Arapahos, and Comanches, was the federal government's first attempt to confine the Plains tribes to reservations and force them to follow the white man's lifestyle. Just a year later, Lieutenant Colonel George Armstrong Custer and the U.S. Seventh Cavalry made a surprise winter attack, destroying Black Kettle's village on the Washita River in present-day western Oklahoma. They killed many Cheyennes,

Colonel John Chivington led the Colorado Volunteer Militia that carried out the Sand Creek Massacre in 1864. The U.S. Congress condemned Colonel Chivington for the massacre.

I have come to kill Indians, and believe it is right and honorable to use any means under God's heaven to kill Indians.

*Colonel John Chivington, 1864*

A Cheyenne record of the Sand Creek Massacre, painted on a buffalo robe. Plains Indians frequently recorded historical events with buffalo-robe paintings.

9

## Black Kettle: A Man Betrayed

One of the few survivors of the Sand Creek Massacre, Black Kettle (about 1803–1868) was a Southern Cheyenne peace chief. His Cheyenne name was Moketavato. He had sought peace with Colonel John Chivington of the Colorado Volunteers, who told him to camp with his people at Sand Creek. When Chivington launched a surprise attack on the peace chief's village, Black Kettle tried to raise the American flag that Chivington had given him, not knowing that it was the same man who was attacking him.

Cheyenne chiefs Dull Knife (seated) and Little Wolf in 1877. The war they waged over the Bozeman Trail remains one of the only wars that the United States ever lost.

including Black Kettle and his wife. By 1869, the Southern Cheyennes were forced to move to a reservation in Indian Territory in what is now Oklahoma.

## War on the Northern Plains

Meanwhile, the Northern Cheyennes, led by Little Wolf and Dull Knife, joined the Lakota Sioux, led by Red Cloud, in the war over the Bozeman Trail in the 1860s. Together, the Indians forced the U.S. Army to abandon the trail to Montana and the three army forts that had been built to protect gold miners who were **trespassing** on Cheyenne and Lakota land.

An Indian painting of the Battle of the Little Bighorn. One week after the Battle of the Rosebud, Northern Cheyennes, led by Brave Wolf and Lame White Man, helped the Lakotas destroy Lieutenant Colonel Custer's cavalry troop on June 24, 1876, at the Battle of the Little Bighorn. The entire United States was stunned.

During the 1870s, Northern Cheyennes again joined the Lakotas in war. The 1868 Treaty of Fort Laramie reserves the Black Hills of South Dakota to the Cheyennes and Lakotas as their sacred lands. When gold was discovered there in 1874, however, the U.S. government sent large armies to protect the prospectors who took the land for their own. In June 1876, Northern Cheyennes and Lakotas shocked U.S. generals invading Cheyenne homelands by turning back the army at the Battle of the Rosebud and wiping out the Seventh Cavalry at the Battle of the Little Big Horn. By the late 1870s, however, the army had forced all the Plains Indians to accept reservation life.

## Lean Bear

A Northern Cheyenne peace chief, Lean Bear (1813–1864), traveled to Washington, D.C., in 1863 and met President Abraham Lincoln. A year later, when he encountered troops led by Colonel John Chivington, Lean Bear attempted to show them his peace medal and papers signed by President Lincoln. Chivington's soldiers shot and killed him.

At boarding schools, Cheyenne children were forced to look, dress, and act like American children and forbidden to speak their own language or practice their religion. They had to do all the work of running the schools, all the cleaning, cooking, and farming, which provided food for the school.

Tepees provided a perfect home for the Cheyennes. They could be taken down quickly, moved many miles away, and then put back up just as quickly.

## Reservation Life

By 1869, the Southern Cheyennes had been forced to share a reservation in western Indian Territory with the Southern Arapahos. There, they endured poverty, sickness, and the U. S. policy of forcing Indians to adopt white values. The U.S. government also suppressed their religious beliefs and practices and made their children attend **boarding schools**.

The U.S. government forced the Northern Cheyennes to move to the Southern Cheyenne reservation, promising they could return to their northern homelands if they didn't like the reservation. The largest group, 937 people, arrived in August 1877. Within two months, two-thirds of them were sick with **malaria**.

When the Northern Cheyennes wanted to return to their homeland, the government denied their request. In 1878, a large group of

Cheyennes left anyway. The army killed many during their journey, but about two hundred reached their old homes. In 1884, a presidential order created the Northern Cheyenne Reservation in southeastern Montana and allowed these Cheyennes to remain.

## Dividing and Selling Cheyenne Land

During the 1880s, the U.S. government forced the Southern Cheyennes to divide their **communal** land into small plots in a process called **allotment**. In 1892, their remaining 3.5 million acres (1.4 million hectares) were opened to white settlers. Northern Cheyennes, however, were able keep control of most of their land. Today, the tribe still owns nearly 97 percent of its reservation.

During the twentieth century, the U.S. government assumed that Native Americans would disappear as a distinct people and **assimilate** into American culture. In 1907, the Southern Cheyennes were forced to become citizens of both the United States and the new state of Oklahoma; no longer part of an independent Indian **nation**, they could not make decisions about the tribe and its future. In 1924, the U.S. Citizenship Act forced the Northern Cheyennes to also become U.S. citizens. It was only during the civil rights movements of the 1960s and 1970s that the U.S. government stopped trying to force Indians to be like white people and allowed them to govern themselves more.

Cheyennes and Arapahos on their reservation in Indian Territory. This photo was taken in 1889 near Fort Reno.

# Traditional Way of Life

## Traditional Woodlands Life

In the Great Lakes woodlands where the tribe first lived, the Cheyennes farmed, fished, and hunted. There, they also made pottery, an art that was lost when they were forced to move to the Great Plains.

## Horses — and Life — on the Plains

When the Cheyennes acquired horses in about 1760, their way of life on the Plains changed dramatically. Before the arrival of horses, Cheyenne camps, including tepees, were moved on small sleds, called travois, made of poles and dragged by dogs. Horses could pull a much larger travois, so tepees could be a lot bigger.

Horses also made buffalo hunting much easier and more productive. Hunters could travel farther and faster in search of buffaloes. With more food, children died less frequently, allowing the Cheyennes to grow into a large and powerful tribe.

A Southern Cheyenne family in 1890. The horse is pulling a travois.

The Cheyennes also became an important link in the chain of horse-trading that made horses readily available to tribes throughout the Great Plains region. Stealing horses from other tribes was also considered a great sport.

## A Useful Animal

The buffalo provided for virtually all the needs of the Cheyennes, not just for food but also for warm robes for winter clothing and blankets. The hides were used to cover tepees and were cut into strips and twisted together to make ropes. Big spoons were carved from the horns, while the sinews were used for bowstrings. Even the hooves were used, boiled to make glue.

The introduction of horses created a golden age for Plains Indians. This painting is by Frederic Remington, a white American who created many paintings of the American West.

The Cheyennes used every part of the buffalo, wasting nothing. Whites, however, slaughtered the buffaloes by the millions just to sell the hide, worth about one dollar each. They left the meat to rot on the Plains. By the 1880s, Americans had destroyed all the great herds of buffaloes. The Cheyennes thus lost their main source of food, leaving them near starvation and forcing them to accept reservation life.

Cheyenne women created beautiful clothing for their families. This shirt is made of tanned hide with colored beadwork. Porcupine quills decorate the handle of this spoon made from a buffalo horn.

A Cheyenne cradle board. Cradle boards allowed a mother to work while her baby remained safe.

## Traditional Cheyenne Childhood

Family life has always been very important to the Cheyenne people. In traditional Cheyenne communities, children are surrounded by relatives of all ages and by elders who take a special interest in the children.

This did not mean, however, that the children were limited in what they could do. On the Plains, Cheyenne children were given great freedom and allowed to make decisions for themselves almost as though they were adults. This was especially true regarding horse riding. From a very early age, Cheyenne boys and girls practically grew up on horseback, becoming amazingly skilled long before they were teenagers.

Around the Cheyenne camps, young boys played with small bows and arrows, shooting at birds. Girls had dolls made by their grandmothers and played house with small tepees that were only about knee-high.

A Cheyenne mother with her child. By carrying the baby on her back, the mother can keep her hands free for other work.

## Courtship and Marriage

When it was time to get married, Cheyenne **courtship** could last as long as five years before the girl would agree to marry. The girl's family arranged some marriages, but many also developed out of dating and courtship. Dating always took place under the watchful eyes of her relatives.

There were no elaborate ceremonies for marriage, mainly an exchange of gifts between the families. Divorce was rare, but it was simple and quick. A woman would put her husband's belongings outside of the tepee, or a man would simply not return to her tepee, saying he had "thrown away his wife."

For this Cheyenne boy, the bow and arrow are more than toys. The rabbits and other small game he brings home will help feed his family.

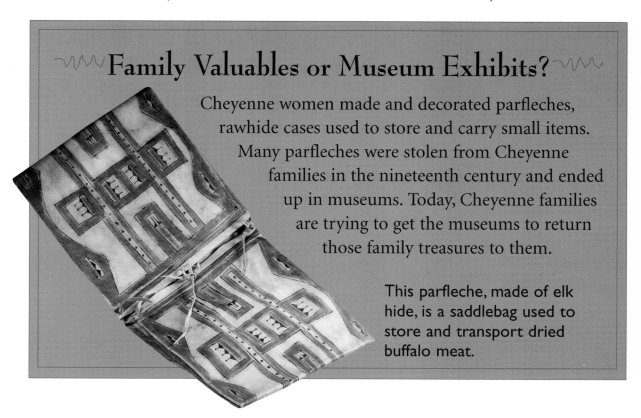

## ᷙᷙᷙFamily Valuables or Museum Exhibits?ᷙᷙᷙ

Cheyenne women made and decorated parfleches, rawhide cases used to store and carry small items. Many parfleches were stolen from Cheyenne families in the nineteenth century and ended up in museums. Today, Cheyenne families are trying to get the museums to return those family treasures to them.

This parfleche, made of elk hide, is a saddlebag used to store and transport dried buffalo meat.

After getting married, the man lived near his wife's relatives. His mother-in-law was forbidden to speak to him or even to look directly at him. She had to talk to him through another person, an arrangement that helped avoid conflict within the family.

## Tribal Government

The Cheyennes became famous for their Council of Forty-Four, a tribal council that originally consisted of four chiefs from each of the eleven Cheyenne bands. As time went by, the number of bands decreased. Some entire bands, for example, were lost during the cholera epidemic of 1849. However, the Cheyennes maintained the tradition of having forty-four members of the council, whose main role was to settle disputes among the Cheyenne people.

A Dog Soldier. Being invited to join the Dog Soldier Society was one of the highest honors a Cheyenne warrior could achieve.

## Social and Military Societies

Matters of war were left to the military societies. Nearly every Cheyenne man belonged to one of numerous different societies, which were like military and social clubs. Sometimes women were allowed to join.

The Dog Soldier Society became probably the most famous group of warriors on the Great Plains in the 1800s. Known for their bravery and skill as fighters, they were among the greatest **light cavalry** in the history of warfare. They led all other Cheyenne warriors into battle. When the tribe moved its camp, they had the high honor and great responsibility of being the rear guard.

Cheyenne women had their own societies. Being allowed to join the Quillers' Society was a high honor. Its members were responsible for maintaining high standards in making the most elaborate clothing decorated with porcupine quills and for instructing young women in the craft.

A Cheyenne painting of the Dog Soldiers. Much of the artwork of the Cheyennes was lost during the Plains wars of the nineteenth century; some of it was stolen and is now shown in museums.

Porcupine quills, some of them dyed, decorated clothing and other items.

## A "Backward" Society

The most remarkable Cheyenne society are the famous Contraries. Its members were required to do most things backward, the opposite of how other people did them. Walking backward and saying good-bye when you meant hello was not a routine that everyone could learn how to do.

## Traditional Cheyenne Beliefs

The Cheyennes believe in a Creator and in an afterlife, which is spent in the Milky Way galaxy of stars. There, Cheyennes join their dead relatives and friends.

The most important religious person in Cheyenne culture was Sweet Medicine, a Cheyenne **prophet** who traveled to Bear Butte in the Black Hills and returned with the Sacred Arrows of the Cheyennes. Bear Butte is a place where Cheyennes go to pray. Since that time, the most important Cheyenne religious event each year is the Renewal of the Sacred Arrows. It takes place in the summer on the longest day of the year. The feathers of the arrows are replaced in the ceremony. During the rest of the year, a Cheyenne elder guards the Sacred Arrows, a position of great responsibility.

## Sacred Medicine Hat

When the Sutaio people merged with the Cheyennes long ago, they brought the Sacred Medicine Hat, another religious item of great significance to the Cheyennes. The Sacred Medicine Hat (sometimes called the Sacred Buffalo Hat) is entrusted to the care of a respected elder of Sutaio tribal descent. The Sutaios also shared with the Cheyennes other religious knowledge and ceremonies that are important parts of Cheyenne life, including the Sun Dance ceremony and the teachings of the Sutaio prophet named Erect Horns.

A Cheyenne buffalo medicine hat. Cheyennes learned medicine-hat rituals many generations ago from the Sutaios.

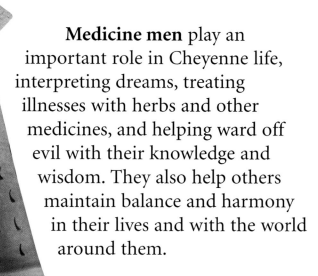

**Medicine men** play an important role in Cheyenne life, interpreting dreams, treating illnesses with herbs and other medicines, and helping ward off evil with their knowledge and wisdom. They also help others maintain balance and harmony in their lives and with the world around them.

The painting and decorations on this buckskin Cheyenne medicine tepee have religious significance.

## The Sun Dance Ceremony

The Cheyenne Sun Dance ceremony each summer is an important time for the tribe. At this ritual, participants renew their promises to work for the benefit of the tribe and for the earth. The ceremonies involve going without food and water for a long time and praying and dancing for several days, all under the guidance of a medicine man who conducts the ceremonies.

Dressed for the Sun Dance, these Cheyenne men were photographed by Edward S. Curtis, a famous photographer of American Indian life, in 1911.

# Today

## Modern Cheyennes

Today, both the Northern and Southern Cheyennes retain and practice many elements of their traditional life. They also share the responsibilities of maintaining and protecting important religious items between the two tribes. The Northern Cheyennes keep the Sacred Medicine Hat, while the Southern Cheyennes guard the Sacred Arrows. The two tribes keep in close contact with each other, visiting frequently and attending each other's ceremonies and powwows.

The Northern Cheyennes operate Dull Knife College, one of the two dozen tribally owned and operated institutions of higher education that make up the American Indian Consortium of Higher Education. The college is located at Lame Deer, Montana.

A young Cheyenne in powwow outfit. Since judges watch many dancers compete at the same time, they track his performance by the number he is wearing.

## Warriors and Leaders

Cheyennes have distinguished themselves in the twentieth century as soldiers in the U.S. armed forces in World War I, World War II, the Korean War, the Vietnam War, and the Gulf War, continuing their proud tradition as gallant fighting men. Cheyennes have also achieved distinction as leaders of political organizations and legislative bodies, including the National Congress of American Indians, where Susan Shown Harjo, a

Southern Cheyenne, served as executive director from 1984 to 1987. In Congress, Ben Nighthorse Campbell, a Northern Cheyenne, was elected to the U.S. Senate from Colorado in 1992.

Many Cheyennes live and work in urban areas throughout the United States, but most continue to live on or near their reservations in Montana and Oklahoma, where their daily lives are very similar to those of other rural Americans. Now that Cheyenne children are no longer sent away to boarding schools, they can live at home with their families and participate in powwows and other tribal activities. They now have educational opportunities that other children have while still being able to maintain their Cheyenne culture. Many Cheyennes have acquired college educations and pursue careers in the professions, working as managers, doctors, lawyers, and teachers.

The Cheyennes in Oklahoma are located at the far eastern edge of the Great Plains, an area that receives much more rain than the high plains farther to the west.

## ∼∿∿ Senator Ben Nighthorse Campbell ∿∿∼

When Ben Nighthorse Campbell (born 1933), a Northern Cheyenne, was elected a senator from Colorado, he became the only American Indian in the U.S. Senate. As a young man, he joined the U.S. Air Force in 1951 and served in the Korean War, learning judo while in Korea. In 1963, he won a gold medal in judo at the Pan-American Games. In 1982, he was elected to the Colorado House of Representatives and, four years later, to the U.S. House of Representatives. He became a U.S. senator in 1992.

# The Northern Cheyennes

The Northern Cheyenne Reservation was increased to its present size of 444,500 acres (180,000 ha) in southeastern Montana by a presidential order in 1900. Bordered on the west by the Crow Reservation and on the east by the Tongue River, the reservation is home to about six thousand of the approximately eight thousand tribal members.

While some of the land consists of steep hills and narrow valleys, much of the reservation is rich grassland and hills. Ranching and farming are the most important economic activities. The tribe also maintains herds of elk and buffalo. The Cheyenne buffalo herd was started in the 1970s and now numbers more than one hundred animals on nearly 4,000 acres (1,600 ha) of grassland. The tribe also manages 90,000 acres (36,400 ha) of forests for harvesting and selling timber.

Cheyenne tepees stand near Lame Deer, Montana, in the Northern Cheyenne Reservation, a place of great natural beauty.

The Northern Cheyennes have refused to allow the mining of rich coal deposits, which were discovered in 1960, on their reservation. They object to the destruction of the land from open-pit mining, which occurs in areas near the reservation. After suffering several generations of being forced to attend boarding schools, the Cheyennes now maintain their own elementary school on the reservation. Older students attend the Morning Star High School.

The two Cheyenne tribes are widely separated. The Northern Cheyenne Reservation lies in southeastern Montana, while the Southern Cheyennes live with the Arapahos on the Concho Reservation in western Oklahoma.

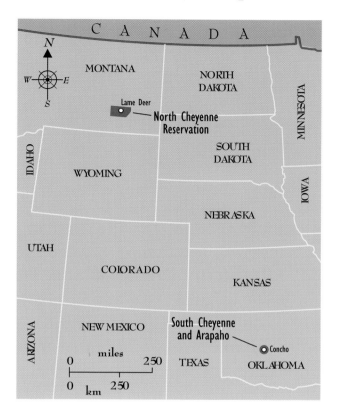

## At Peace at Last

In 1879, U.S. Army soldiers killed thirty-one Cheyenne warriors at Hat Creek Bluffs on the northern Great Plains. Instead of allowing the Cheyennes to bury their dead relatives, the Army Medical Museum seized the bodies, kept them in boxes, and then proceeded to forget about them. It took more than one hundred years for the Cheyenne people to recover the bodies of their relatives. In October 1993, the bodies were finally returned to the Cheyennes under the Native American Graves Protection and Repatriation Act of 1990.

A Southern Cheyenne in traditional dress wears a headdress made of feathers.

## The Southern Cheyennes

Since 1869, the Southern Cheyennes have been joined with the Southern Arapahos on the Concho Reservation on the edge of the Great Plains in western Oklahoma. Known as the Cheyenne-Arapaho Tribes of Oklahoma, the two tribes govern the reservation by a joint business committee composed of representatives elected from both tribes under a **constitution** adopted in 1937.

## Reducing the Land and Tribe

The original reservation consisted of more than 5 million acres (2,024,000 ha). Today, only 85,000 acres (34,400 ha) remain in tribal control. Most of the land that was individually assigned to tribal members in the late nineteenth century soon passed into white hands, often by **fraud**, against which the Cheyennes were given no protection by the courts. During the 1950s, the Southern Cheyennes had to fight attempts by the U.S. Bureau of Indian Affairs and the U.S. Congress to end the status of their tribe as an independent nation and relocate their people to urban areas in distant cities in the United States.

## A People Recover

Today, the combined population of the Southern Cheyennes and Southern Arapahos is about ten thousand, of which about half live on the Concho Reservation. Many of the others live in Oklahoma City and other urban areas in the region.

Farming and cattle raising are important economic activities. A tribally owned **casino** provides both employment for tribal members and income for tribal programs, such as health care and education.

Both the Northern and Southern Cheyenne people are adjusting to the great changes they have endured during the past century. They are now taking control of their lives, rather than having their lives controlled by the U.S. government. The Cheyenne people are moving confidently into the twenty-first century.

Southern Cheyennes in Oklahoma. Cheyenne young people have a brighter future today than at any time during the past century.

## Freedom of Religion

The Native American Church, which uses a drug called peyote in its religious ceremonies, has a strong following among both the Northern and Southern Cheyennes. For many years, federal and state authorities tried to put Indians who practiced the religion of the Native American Church in jail for using peyote. Now a special law protects the religious use of peyote, which is obtained from a cactus, by members of the church.

# Time Line

| | |
|---|---|
| **before 1700** | Cheyennes live in the Great Lakes region. |
| **about 1700** | Cheyennes' enemies, the Ojibwes and the Assiniboins, drive the Cheyennes toward the west onto the Great Plains. |
| **about 1760** | Cheyennes acquire horses. |
| **about 1800** | Cheyennes merge with the Sutaio tribe. |
| **early 1800s** | Cheyennes trade buffalo robes to American traders; Sioux drive the Cheyennes farther west. |
| **1825** | Cheyennes sign first treaty with the United States. |
| **1832** | Cheyennes divide into Northern and Southern Cheyennes. |
| **1851** | Cheyennes sign Treaty of Fort Laramie. |
| **1856** | U.S. Army destroys a Cheyenne village, igniting a long war. |
| **1864** | Sand Creek Massacre. |
| **1868** | Colonel George Custer and the cavalry kill Black Kettle. |
| **1869** | Southern Cheyennes are forced to live on reservation. |
| **1872** | Southern Cheyenne children are forced into boarding schools. |
| **1876** | Battle of the Little Bighorn in Montana. |
| **1877** | Northern Cheyennes are forced to move to Southern Cheyenne reservation in Indian Territory. |
| **1878** | Northern Cheyennes flee from the southern reservation. |
| **1880s** | Southern Cheyennes are forced to accept land allotments. |
| **1884** | Northern Cheyenne Reservation is established. |
| **1892** | Remaining 3.5 million acres (1.4 million ha) of Southern Cheyenne Reservation sold to white settlers. |
| **1900** | Northern Cheyenne Reservation is enlarged to present size. |
| **1937** | Southern Cheyennes adopt tribal constitution with Arapahos. |
| **1950s** | Southern Cheyennes fight American efforts to terminate them as a tribe and move their people to distant cities. |
| **1970s** | Northern Cheyennes begin building a herd of buffalo. |
| **1992** | Ben Nighthorse Campbell is elected to Senate from Colorado. |

# Glossary

**alcoholism:** a disease in which people's desire to drink alcohol is so strong they cannot control it.

**alien:** not familiar, different.

**allotment:** the act of dividing land and forcing Native Americans to accept individual ownership of small farms, rather than all of the Indian land being owned by the tribe as a whole.

**assimilate:** to force one group to adopt the culture — the language, lifestyle, and values — of another.

**boarding schools:** places where students must live at the school.

**casino:** a building that has slot machines, card games, and other gambling games.

**cholera:** a deadly disease that causes vomiting, diarrhea, and cramps.

**communal:** owned by a group of people rather than by individuals.

**constitution:** the basic laws and principles of a nation that outline the powers of the government and the rights of the people.

**courtship:** a period when men and women consider getting married.

**epidemic:** a widespread outbreak of any serious disease.

**fraud:** an act of tricking or cheating.

**immigrants:** people who are moving to a new home, usually far away.

**light cavalry:** warriors or soldiers trained to fight on horseback.

**malaria:** a deadly disease that causes chills, high fevers, and sweating.

**massacre:** a brutal killing of many people.

**medicine men:** healers and spiritual leaders.

**nation:** people who have their own customs, laws, and land separate from other nations or peoples.

**nomadic:** moving from place to place often.

**prophet:** a person who tells what will happen in the future.

**treaty:** an agreement among two or more nations.

**trespassing:** entering someone's land without permission.

# More Resources

## Web Sites:

**http://www.cheyenne-arapaho.nsn.us** The official web site of the Cheyenne and Arapaho tribes of Oklahoma. Click on *culture* to find out more about Cheyenne culture and history.

**http://www.nps.gov/fola/indians/htm** A description of the Fort Laramie Treaty and the tribes living around the fort, including the Cheyenne Indians.

**http://www.pbs.org/weta/thewest/program/episodes/one/dog_soldiers.htm** Briefly describes Dog Soldiers and the prophet Sweet Medicine. You can also search **www.pbs.org** for other information on the Cheyenne people.

## Videos:

*Paha Sapa: The Struggle for the Black Hills.* Mystic Fire Video, 1993.

## Books:

Bonvillain, Nancy. *The Cheyennes: People of the Plains.* Millbrook Press, 1996.

Henry, Christopher E. *Ben Nighthorse Campbell: Cheyenne Chief and U.S. Senator.* Chelsea House, 1994.

Limberhand, Dennis, and Mary Em Parrilli. *Indian Nations: The Cheyenne.* Raintree Steck-Vaughn, 2001.

Meli, Franco. *A Cheyenne* (Day With). Runestone Press, 2000.

Nashoba, Nuchi. *Ben Nighthorse Campbell: Senator and Artist.* Modern Curriculum Press, 1994.

Sneve, Virginia Driving Hawk. *The Cheyennes: A First Americans Book.* Holiday House, 1996.

Viola, Herman J. *It Is a Good Day to Die: Indian Eyewitnesses Tell the Story of the Battle of the Little Bighorn.* Crown Publishers, 1998.

# Things to Think About and Do

## Life with Horses

How many reasons can you think of to explain why nomadic people who travel a lot would find that horses make their wandering lifestyle a lot easier? List those reasons.

## Your Life at Boarding School

How would your school days be different if you were sent away from home and forced to live in a boarding school where nobody spoke English, where you had to help do all the cooking and cleaning at the school, and where you were not allowed to have much contact with your family?

## Is a People's Heritage for Display?

Have you ever wondered how museums got the Indian things that are on display? Can you think of any reasons why Indian people might not be happy about some of the things that are in museums? Write an essay about your thoughts.

# Index